Let's Go! Let's Grow!

WHAT IS SPROUTING?

Stephanie Anne Box

Rourke
Educational Media

A Division of
Carson Dellosa
Education

Before Reading: *Building Background Knowledge and Vocabulary*

Building background knowledge can help children process new information and build upon what they already know. Before reading a book, it is important to tap into what children already know about the topic. This will help them develop their vocabulary and increase their reading comprehension.

Questions and Activities to Build Background Knowledge:

1. Look at the front cover of the book and read the title. What do you think this book will be about?
2. What do you already know about this topic?
3. Take a book walk and skim the pages. Look at the table of contents, photographs, captions, and bold words. Did these text features give you any information or predictions about what you will read in this book?

Vocabulary: *Vocabulary Is Key to Reading Comprehension*

Use the following directions to prompt a conversation about each word.
- Read the vocabulary words.
- What comes to mind when you see each word?
- What do you think each word means?

Vocabulary Words:
- *leaves*
- *nutrients*
- *seedling*
- *stem*

During Reading: *Reading for Meaning and Understanding*

To achieve deep comprehension of a book, children are encouraged to use close reading strategies. During reading, it is important to have children stop and make connections. These connections result in deeper analysis and understanding of a book.

 Close Reading a Text

During reading, have children stop and talk about the following:
- Any confusing parts
- Any unknown words
- Text to text, text to self, text to world connections
- The main idea in each chapter or heading

Encourage children to use context clues to determine the meaning of any unknown words. These strategies will help children learn to analyze the text more thoroughly as they read.

When you are finished reading this book, turn to the last page for an **After-Reading** activity.

Table of Contents

Sowing Seeds

What is sprouting?

How are these seeds the same? How are they different? What do you think will sprout?

Most plants begin as seeds. A seed is a living thing. Seeds come from the flower of a plant. They are different shapes, sizes, and colors.

Every seed has a seed coat. It protects the seed. Can you find one?

Seeds are planted, dropped, or blown by the wind. Roots grow into the soil. They hold the seeds in place and take in **nutrients**.

How do roots
help a plant?

The seed germinates. A **stem** reaches for the sun. It grows leaves.

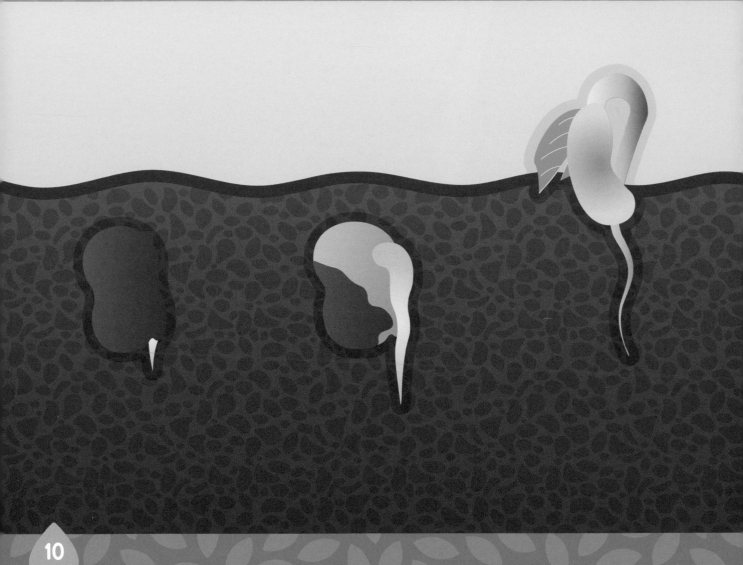

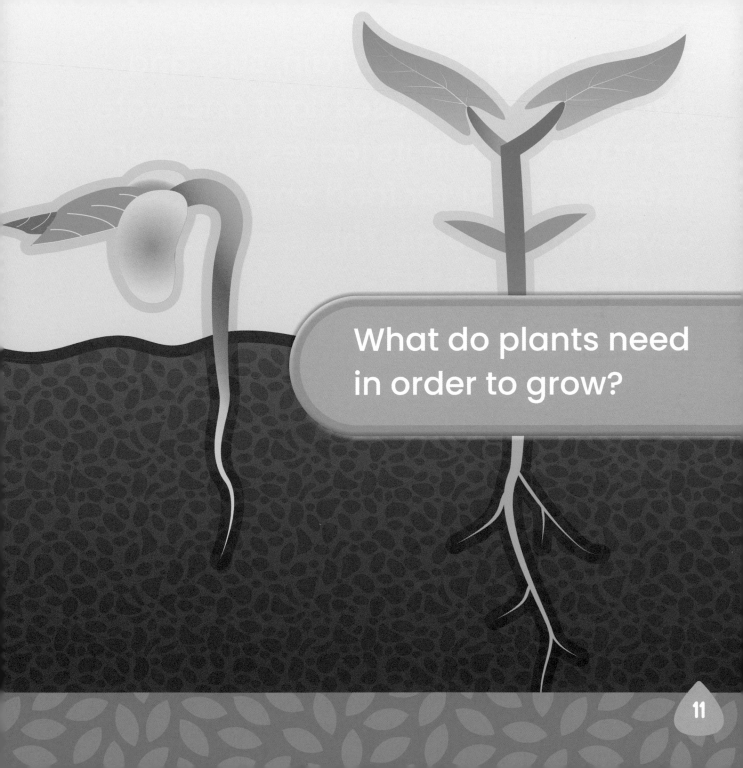

What do plants need in order to grow?

The **seedling** takes in rain, sun, and carbon dioxide. It uses light and water to make sugar in its leaves. The plant uses the sugar for food and releases oxygen into the air. This is called photosynthesis.

Why is a plant green? Plants have chlorophyll. Chlorophyll helps the plant make food and makes the plant green.

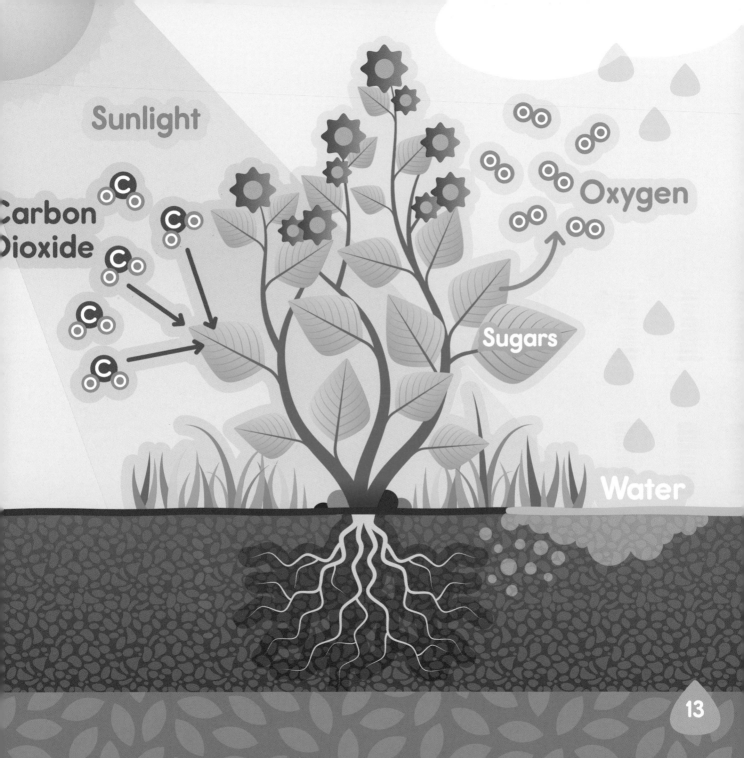

Sunlight

Carbon Dioxide

Oxygen

Sugars

Water

13

Plants live all over the world. They grow and change. Plants produce flowers, fruit, or both.

Fruit

Stem →

Flower

Leaves

Roots

There are five parts of a plant.

We eat plants, use them to build, and even wear them.

Plants give us oxygen to breathe.
People couldn't live without plants.

Some medicines
are made from plants.

Look what sprouted! Think back to the beginning. Did you guess correctly?

Photo Glossary

leaves (leevz): Flat and usually green structures attached to stems and growing from branches of a tree or stems of a plant.

nutrients (NOO-tree-uhnts): Substances such as proteins, minerals, or vitamins that are needed by people, animals, and plants to stay strong and healthy.

seedling (SEED-ling): A young plant that has been grown from a seed rather than a cutting.

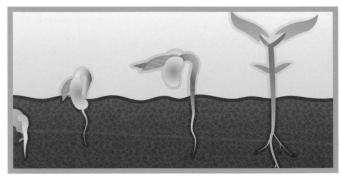

stem (stem): The main, upward growing part of a plant from which the leaves and flowers grow; the stalk.

Activity: Grow Your Own Window Seed

Supplies

Wet paper towel
Clear zipper sandwich bag
Dry pinto or lima bean
Tape
Window with natural light

Directions:

Place a dry bean on top of a wet paper towel. Place in a clear zipper sandwich bag. Tape the bag to a window with natural light. Do not close the zipper. Watch the bean sprout roots, a stem, and leaves. You will notice the seed coat leave once it is no longer needed. (Note: You may need to spray the paper towel with water if it dries out during the 3-to-5-day growing process.)

Index

About the Author

Stephanie Anne Box loves plants but doesn't have a green thumb—she tends to overwater them! Stephanie is a kindergarten teacher who lives in Mississippi with her husband, Josh, and her dog, Dudley.

After-Reading Activity

Track your plants! Make a list of the foods you ate for lunch. Are the foods seeds, stems, leaves, flowers, or fruits?

Library of Congress PCN Data

What Is Sprouting? / Stephanie Anne Box
(Let's Go! Let's Grow!)
ISBN 978-1-73165-178-5 (hard cover)(alk. paper)
ISBN 978-1-73165-223-2 (soft cover)
ISBN 978-1-73165-193-8 (e-Book)
Library of Congress Control Number: 1234567890

Rourke Educational Media
Printed in the United States of America
01-3402111937

www.rourkeeducationalmedia.com

Edited by: Laura Malay
Cover design by: Tammy Ortner
Interior design by: Tammy Ortner
Photo Credits: Cover p 1 © MP_P, © AVN Photo Lab, © Ivaylo Ivanov, © Filip Dokladal, © Katharina Scharle, p 4 © Elvira Tursynbayeva, p 5 © Ruth Swan, © ILYA AKINSHIN, © florin Oprea, p 6 © ChWeiss, p 8 © Ivaylo Ivanov, p 9 © Anest, p 10,11© Nasky, p 12 © Ulrich22, p 13 © VectorMine, p 14 © Peredniankina, © gresei, © Pi-Lens, © Rostislav Stefanek, p 15 © Kazakova Maryia, p 16 © Creativa Images, p 17 © Leszek Glasner, © Khosrork, p 18 © SeventyFour, p 19 © Pixel-Shot, p 20 © ArTDi101, p 21 © barmalini, © uly.u.v, p 22 © ulrich22, © Ivaylo Ivanov, © Elvira Tursynbayeva, © Nasky p 24 © Joan Peno McCool